Get-A-Long Poems

And Other Conundrums of Childhood

by

Dr. Beverly Kastelic Long

MainSpring Books

Printed in the United States of America

ISBN 979-8-89114-055-4 (sc)
ISBN 979-8-89114-056-1 (e)

Library of Congress Control Number: 2024901371

2024.03.05

MainSpring Books
5901 W. Century Blvd
Suite 750
Los Angeles, CA, US, 90045

www.mainspringbooks.com

Illustrator Bios

Born and raised in Western Pennsylvania, Joseph Ezra Durick was formally educated at Penn State University and holds two degrees in engineering. In 2009, Ezra was given the opportunity to apply his experience in 3-D design and construction through an apprenticeship as a tattoo artist. He continues to use that training along with inspiration from other amazing artists to push his creativity in the design of custom tattoos.

Craig Hubert, who was born and raised in Hyde Park, Pennsylvania, has always been interested in art and started out as an illustrator of comic books. He has been tattooing since 2005, and is currently the owner of the Iron Element Tattoo Gallery. Craig shares his love of gardening and golf with his wife Melissa and his son Tyler.

Get-A-Long

Get along! my teacher warned,
If you want to keep a job.
And so I searched both high and low,
And got my brother Bob.

Get along! my father said,
With family and with friends.
And so I went to Auntie's house,
And got my brother Ben.

Get along! the mayor begged,
If you're living on this hill.
I jogged down to the corner store,
And got my brother Bill.

Their tempers flared,
They all were mad,
They said I'd gone quite wrong.
What would you do
If you were me,
And YOUR last name was Long?

Run, Gypsies, Run

The gypsies took my sister,
Beth, It happened late one day.
While digging in the flower box,
They carried her away.

We tried to track my sister down,
And followed her clear trail.
We found the neighbor's old tom cat,
With ketchup on his tail.

We hurried fast across the street,
To see if she was hiding.
But all we found were two old goats,
My sister had been riding.

We drove four times around the block,
To try to find a clue.
We found her hat, her shirt, two socks,
And one quite soaked right shoe.

We knocked on each and every door,
And walked a dozen miles.
How odd that when they heard of Beth,
Our neighbors were all smiles.

The gypsies are a clever lot,
No wisdom do they lack.
And so, before we could protest,
They brought my sister back!

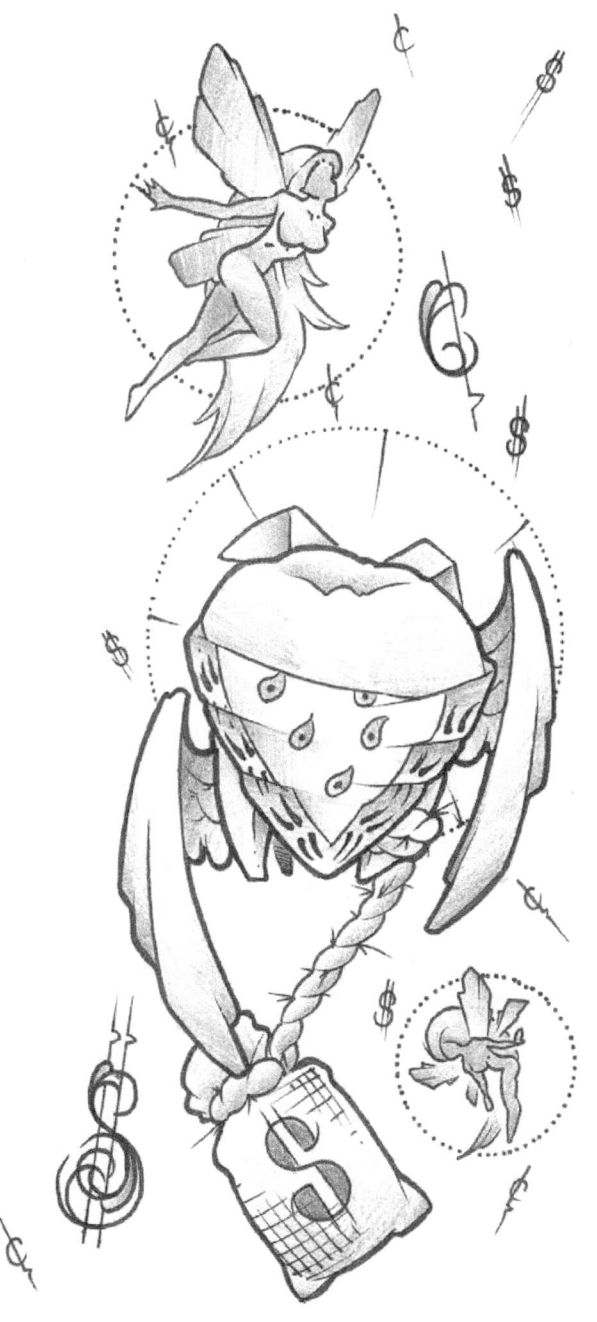

A Matter of Crime

I know that she is just a fairy,
But stealing teeth is kind of scary!

What made her start this life of crime,
Of taking teeth and leaving dimes?

Had she no parental supervision?
Did she watch too much television?

I know that she should start today—
Give back the teeth and mend her ways.
But I would not mind a delay.

My teeth are loose and
CRIME DOES PAY!

Messes of Tresses

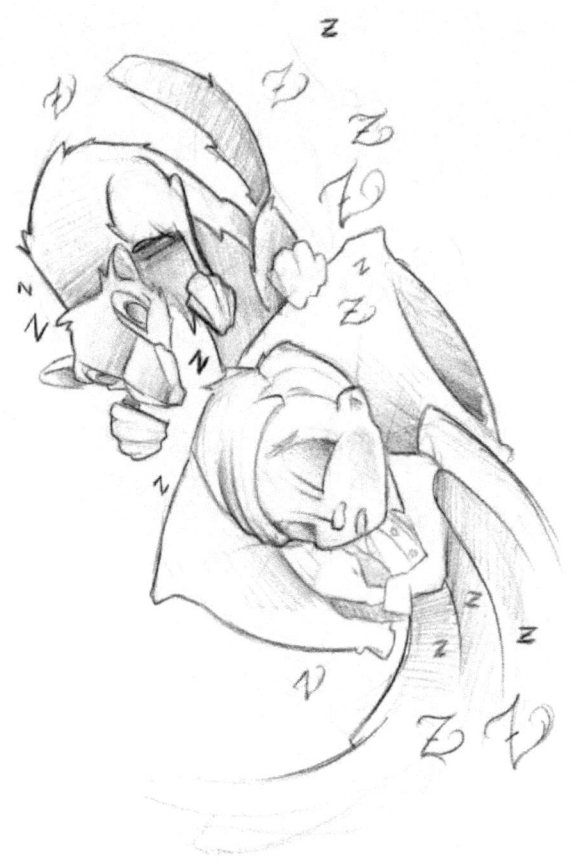

We've tried everything we know—
Locks and bolts and snares.
To keep our house secure from pests,
Like ants and bats and bears.

And yet each morning it is clear
To anyone who cares,
That weasels, wild and wonderful
Have danced through Benny's hair,

We've gathered all the evidence,
That we would ever dare.
Photos show Ben scrubbed and coiffed
When climbing up the stairs.

Mom would gladly testify
His hair is combed just right.
When she kisses Benny's cheek
And tucks him in each night.

And Dad has even taken pains
To peek in unannounced,
To see if Benny's tossed and turned
Or flipped or twirled or bounced.

We've finally just resigned ourselves
Aside from super glue,
That weasels will mess Benny's hair
No matter what we do.

Play it Again, Bob!

Brother Bob's become quite ill—
It really does concern us.
An unknown illness just cropped up
Called play-piano-itis.

The symptoms really are quite strange
We learn more every day.
His hands get stiff and just won't work
When he sits down to play.

It may be just an allergy
To ivory in the keys.
His fingers are both strong and swift
When climbing through the trees.

"It's physical," the doctor said,
"His elbow bend's not right."
Although his elbows bend just fine
At dinner every night.

No medicine has yet been found
To cure my brother's ills.
My parents have tried poultices,
And vitamins and pills.

The only balm poor Bob has found
To which he will surrender,
Is when my Mom at last declares
No lessons till September!

help Me Out at the Ballgame

They took me out to the ballgame,
And I got lost in the crowd.
I was looking for peanuts and crackerjack,
I lost my seat, and I couldn't get back.

Did I hoot? Yes, I did—then I hollered!
I screamed and I yelled without shame.

But—at last!
Hooray!
Dad grabbed my hand And we watched the game.

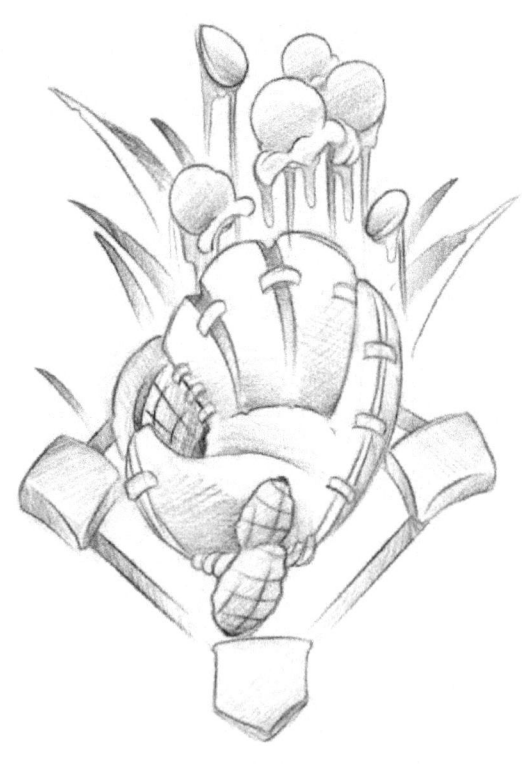

Night Scares

No one knows how Brother Bill
Got it in his head,
That two wild wolves with pointed teeth
Were underneath his bed.

He started sleeping fitfully
A tossin' and a turnin',
And nothing Mom or Dad could say
Could really seem to calm him.

The family searched both high and low
But never could quite say,
That they had ever seen the wolves
By night or light of day.

And though he'd really never seen
The wolves that prowled beneath,
Bill drew us pictures by the score
Of pointed, fang-like teeth.

You may be asking, as I have
If I had used my head,
To tell Bill all about the wolves
Underneath his bed.

Jeepers! Peepers!

Mr. Peepers, Four-Eyes, Googles,
What will they decide to say?
To my little brother Benny
Who got glasses just today?

Squinty, Blind Eyes, Winky-Blinky,
Those are the names they'd call.
As when he was playing third base
Benny couldn't see the ball.

WOW! Amazing! Okey Dokey!
Ben's delighted now to see,
That what he thought were space invaders
Turned out to be a tree.

Dot-To-Dot

My brother, Bill, has never been the kind to play with games.
GO FISH! is just too wild, he says, and SOLITAIRE'S too tame.

Even games that seem quite smart, he doesn't want to try—
Crossword puzzles make him cross, and SCRABBLE makes him cry.

So just imagine our surprise when chicken pox he got,
To find out that our brother, Bill, was good at DOT-TO-DOT!

Chair-O-Batics

Gosh, how daring
Balancing there,
On just one leg
Of the kitchen chair.
Will you crash
Or stay aloft?
'Hope your landing's
Safe and soft!

Misfortune Cookies

Beth and Benny and Billy and Bob,
Went to town to look for a job.
They got a job cooking Chinese food,
But they all got fired 'cos Benny was rude!

Cover Up

I scraped my knee on our front stair,
Mother put a Band-Aid THERE. ☜

I climbed the fence and caught my ear,
Auntie put a Band-Aid HERE. ☜

I fell like Jack and broke my crown,
Grammy put a Band-Aid down. ☟

I had my nose chewed by the pup,
Father put a Band-Aid UP. ☝

I stubbed my toe in bed last night,
Sister put a Band-Aid RIGHT. ☜

I knocked heads with Cousin Jeff,
Brother put a Band-Aid LEFT. ☜

It's raining buckets, but I don't care,
My Band-Aids keep me dry out there!

Sock Monkey Hop

There's a monkey on the table!
Said my Father's sister, Mabel.
He'll eat pancakes if he's able,
Get that monkey off the table!

There's a monkey on my chair!
Yelled my Uncle's daughter, Claire.
It might bite and pull my hair,
Get that monkey off the chair!

There's a monkey on my bed!
That is what my brother said.
So I bonked him on the head,
No more monkey on the bed!

Pox On You

My sister, Beth, has chicken pox,
I don't know how she got 'em.
She never played with chickens much,
My parents never bought 'em.

But chicken pox is what she has,
The doctor says he's certain!
It makes her jump and scream and itch,
And Mother climb the curtain.

I'm glad **I** don't have chicken pox—
I think it would be horrid.
To have small chickens on your head,
And arms and legs and forehead.

My Dad says there are other poxes,
Small and cow, to name a few.
I hope I can't get one of them—
Did I just hear a MOO?

Flip Flop

On Christmas day, with paper flying,
Bill's heart went flip-flop,
'Cos in his final Santa gift,
He found his own lap top.

A computer is the only way,
To keep his grades tip-top.
Bill really must have made his case,
'Cos he got his own lap top.

Once in a while, he must admit,
He downloads some hip hop.
But mostly he's become a geek,
Who has his own lap top.

Mother Goose Unfurled

While napping softly on the bed
With golden ringlets 'round her head,

Beth's window came a bit ajar
And magic breezes from afar,

Swirled through the pages of her book
And gave the poems a different look,

So now we all can have some fun
And see what rhymes have come undone.

Along Came a Muffet

Gently swinging in the breeze,
Over my small tuffet.
Not expecting anyone,
Let alone a Muffet.

Uninvited, down she sat,
Bold as bold could be.
Just the smell of curds and whey
Were enough to frighten me.

I came down to set a spell,
Just to be polite.
And learned arachnophobia
Is not a pretty sight.

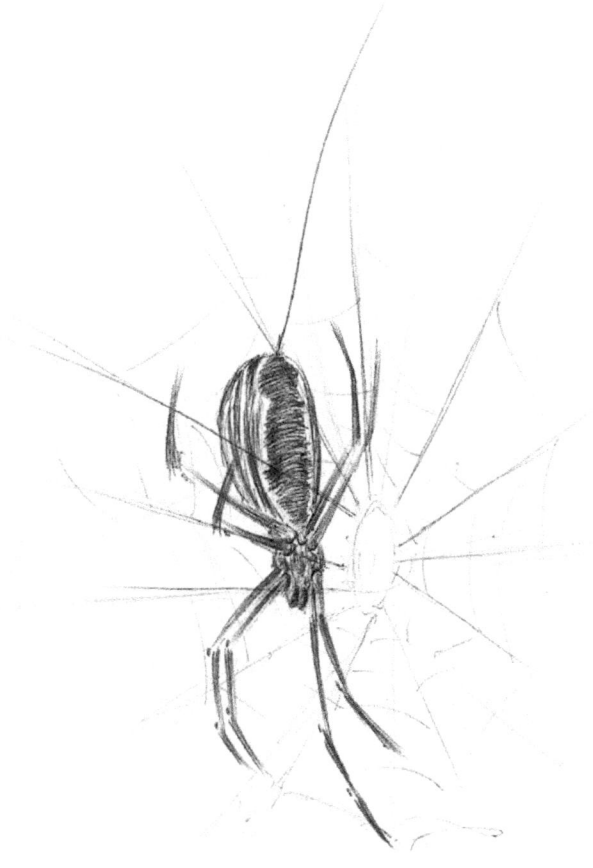

Eggs-actly

There I sat up on the wall,
Never thinking I could fall.
Till those king's men were horsing 'round,
Now here I lie, cracked and on the ground.

You'd think they'd be a clever lot,
But all those king's men—they are not!
A tiny bit of super glue,
Is all they'd really have to do.

They hemmed and hawed
Then here they ran,
With butter and a frying pan.

Jill and Jack

Jill and Jack
They made a pact
To go and find some water.

That they could label, stamp, and sell
In small, designer bottles.

Their plan was nipped
When they were tripped
With EPA red tape.

They've changed their ways
Selling on eBay
Vinegar in brown paper.

Lullaby Alibi

I'm innocent
As I can be.
I struck no mice
Not one—not three!

I think that
I've been very kind
And really paid the mice no mind.
As they've run up and down my belly
With sticky feet all smeared with jelly.

If mice were struck
Then that is that!
Don't look at me—
Go ask the cat.

Mistress Mary

Mary's really not contrary
Although it may appear,
That she frets about her garden
All throughout the year.

In the winter she debates
If she should fertilize,
While in the summer she observes
Her garden's height and size.

Silver bells and cockleshells
She's planted in a row,
But jelly beans and black-eyed peas
Are scattered to and fro.

Mittens Schmittens

Let's make one thing very clear:
The mittens were not lost, my dear.

And certainly not in sets of three—
My siblings did the same as me.

We traded mittens with no ilk,
For bottles full of chocolate milk.

How were we to realize
That with no mittens, there'd be no pies?

Pluto's Revenge

Pluto, Pluto please don't wail,
That as a planet you did fail
To be the size that you should be,
To impress astronomy.
Just be content to be a star,
And twinkle, twinkle as you are.

Pluto, Pluto did you hear?
You ARE a planet now my dear!
The scientist who did you wrong,
Is singing now a different song.
So as a planet you will stay,
But not the farthest one away.

Shoe Shopping

There was a young lady
Who'd lived in a shoe,
With her mother and siblings
Of twenty and two.

She finally was ready
To leave her safe nest,
But just couldn't figure
Which home would be best.

She hired an agent
To take her to places,
That had a great kitchen
And wide, open spaces.

She finally decided
Once she'd seen one or two,
That a black, high-top sneaker
Is the one that would do.

Spider Power

With every little hint of rain
The spider would wash down the drain.

"My size is what is stopping me
From getting to the top," said he.

And so he hatched a clever plan
To make himself a "manly man."

He lifted berries, nuts, and twigs
To make his muscles strong and big.

So now when rain comes pouring down
The little spider stands his ground.

Then marches bravely up the spout
And never, ever washes out.

Tails Be Told

I'm just a frazzled farmer's wife
Busy carving with my knife
I can't take time to stop and see
That no blind mouse, or two, or three
Are running quickly 'cross the table
And don't appear to be quite able
To keep their tails from being whacked
Or body parts from being hacked.

If safety is the issue here
A seeing-eye dog should be near!

Udderly hopeless

Right in the middle
Of the cat and his fiddle
Plinking a merry tune.

The cow in the stable
Believed she was able
To jump right over the moon.

Spoon said to the dish
Do you think that her wish
Will be easy as cutting through butter?

Little dog's laughing halted
When the cow quickly vaulted
And just cleared the moon by an udder.